Gleanings

Poems of the Writers Consortium

Victor Klimoski, Editor

Prior Avenue Publications
Saint Paul, Minnesota

2017

ISBN-13: 9781975977429
ISBN-10: 1975977424
Printed in the USA by Createspace.com

Cover: *The Gleaners* (1857), Jean-Francois Millet
© Shutterstock.com

Back Cover Photo: Sheila Martin

Introduction

When we began meeting as a group over a year ago, it was an act of faith. We did not know each other very well except for a brief workshop series on writing at the Selim Center of the University of St. Thomas. Some of us were experienced writers while others were just beginning to explore this way of interpreting their life experience. Each month without fail, we would meet and share our work, talking about the practice and learning from one another. Ah, there was the greatest reward: mutual learning. While we know that each person sees the world in a unique way, the impact of that truth becomes vivid when someone helps us see into our own story and the way we use words to describe it.

While at first we had no need of a group name, our decision to take on this project of producing a collection changed that. "Consortium" turned out to be a good fit for two reasons. First, it describes a group formed around a common purpose. When applied to business, a consortium has certain rights and obligations each member upholds. While the members of the Writers Consortium do not think in legal terms, we do have several tacit obligations. We are faithful to one another in our monthly sessions because we recognize that in those brief moments of communion something happens that does not happen as readily when we each work in our mental garret. We are also compassionately honest with each other, knowing that feedback has its best impact when we think with the writer and with deep respect for what the writer is seeking to say.

There is a second meaning of *consortium*, however, that is even more compelling for us. A consortium recognizes that its purpose is beyond any one member's resources. No one can write for us. That hard work is ours alone. But gathered together we discover the encouragement, insight, and capacity to push beyond the obstacles every writer confronts. Whether we call it writer's

1

block, a fear of being "no good at all," a self-perceived set of limitations, or the sirens of busyness and distraction, the Consortium calls each of us to a recommitment to the talents we have.

We chose the title *Gleanings* for the collection in part because of the Jean Millet masterpiece. We like to think of ourselves as good stewards of the lives we have been given – stewards of the opportunities and challenges, the blessings and tragedies, the insights and the questions yet to be pondered. At this stage of life, we are not resting but continuing to explore what life has taught us and continues to teach us each day.

Each section of this collection contains the poems selected by the author and critiqued by the group. We listened to the writer's words and the source of each poem. We probed, suggested, wondered aloud. In the final stage, I agreed to serve as the coordinating editor and to use my experience as one final way to "see" into the poem as an objective companion. The opening poem for each section is the author's reflection on the spirit out of which she or he writes.

Writing is a source of joy as much as it is an artistic discipline. Our life together as a writing group has been both. Each of us have learned ways to approach writing that expand our capacity to speak our truth. And the trust we have in each other, undergirded by a shared recognition in the soulful work writing often is, gives us great pleasure.

Victor Klimoski
December, 2017

2

Contents

*

SHEILA MARTIN

Whispers of the Truth

There is always something more trying to push its way to the surface of my life. My soul already knows this! In every moment there are whispers of truth to be heard. My pen often becomes the spokeswoman of these truths. And so, I set her tip against the paper to write. Sometimes there are dark clouds, sometimes, the irregular flutter of the butterfly, sometimes just the directions printed on a box. At first, I let the anxiety of mystery hold the pen. Then, the words slide, slowly, onto the paper, under my captive awe. Then I'm released from captivity, and a torrent falls to the paper. At times, it is not my place, nor do I have the power, to stop it. Eventually, the words dwindle to a drip. Part of me resists that moment, thinking that I can squeeze more words into existence. But the creative spirit doesn't easily listen to such vanity. The poem, in its first form and by its own will, is ready to rest. Whether tentative or strong-willed, the drafting of the poem gives me peace. As the ink dries, a spiritual "Ahhh" blooms in me and makes me happy. Sometimes, I want a birth announcement: "A poem, packed full of both wonderful and recognizable goodness, has survived its birthing!!"

What It Seems To Be

Silence hovering, they sit
together on the well-worn loveseat,
close enough to be available for each other.
Their bent fingers, softened by uselessness,
gently entwined.
The sweetness in this
is all they have left to give.
Eyes, drooped shut, avoiding the familiarity
of shadows and brightness,
and the carpet's matted pathways.
There is finally no need to decide
what color to paint the room.
Newcomers to their rusty lives
believe the conspicuous sweetness
is all there has ever been.
No longer are caustic-edged words flung,
and self-centered tantrums splayed out
on the floor between them.
Their huffs of exasperation have dissipated,
 into the dust of years.

Coarse and Honest Hues

The rusty swing set is still there,
at the edge of the unkempt back yard,
where wind and weeds have been relentless.
The metal frame,
once taller than a child's reach,
remains erect, though slightly askew,
as the soil upon which it sits
has given way.
Its enameled colors, once resplendent
red and bright blue, have faded
to the coarse and honest hues of rust.
No more purposes adorn the frame;
broken from over-use,
broken from lack of use.

What remains of her?
The endurable, willful, steel.
Her relatedness to all that has been around her.
She stayed true.
The children climbed the close-by fence;
curiosity led them away.
She knows no other use,
than to be a swing set.
She knows no other place, than here,
at the edge of the unkempt back yard.

Grazing Presence

There's been an elephant in my pasture,
nonchalantly grazing,
for quite some time.
She's been over there,   on the far distant edge,
up against the sloping ragged forest.
She wasn't very noticeable,
and easy to pay no mind,
my ongoing life being grazed over here.
To my surprise,
despite my knowing of such phenomena,
I felt the rumble of a tectonic shift.
And then, another.
Now, the elephant,
still nonchalantly grazing,
is right next to me and my ongoing life.
She didn't move; my life did.
Does anyone else notice her? Should I point her out?
Does her presence in my pasture
mean anything to anyone, but me?
Can I try to hide her?
 Where can one hide an elephant?
Besides, even if I could,
I'd still know that she's here in my pasture,
still sharing my ongoing life.

Quiver

Within the delicate web,

the quiver on one thread

is felt as tremble,

oh, so fearfully.

> When one hurts,
> when even one struggles,
> we all hurt,
> we all struggle.

The tremble is absorbed

into the far thread too,

oh, so tenderly.

> When one heals,
> when even one is freed,
> we all heal,
> we all are freed.

Step into the Woods

As I step into the woods, the dew
that saturates the verdant floor,
clings to my shoes.
Shards of morning's light
pierce their way through
the canopy of treetops.
The warming light greets me
as it reaches between the dressed branches,
downcast fingers in lacey gloves
bearing nourishment
for the understory of the woods.
A tree's weakest branch,
felled by a cleansing wind,
lies askew on my borrowed deer path.
It now hosts shy and patient lichen.
The odors of decay
constantly rumble, as background.
The optimistic oriole, and chickadee too,
proclaim themselves.
Hopefully, I am a guest
of no consequence.

The Edge of a World

Ever notice
the delicate touch of a fly
turning the page
of a Kindle?
Ever behold
an ever-busy hummingbird,
perched still and preening
on a pine tree branch?
Ever look
at the shy portion
of the morning's sliver moon,
unable to brightly reflect
the sun's emerging rays?
Somewhere out there
lies the edge of a world,
recognizable, and understood.
Here, just now,
mystery abounds,
to blind, and then
to provide a glimpse.

What Does Matter?

At the end of it
we simply die.
It won't matter
if I fluffed the pillow
this morning, or not.
It won't matter
if you brushed your teeth
for the second time today.
It won't matter
if we finally agreed to cut
the grass every Friday.
Life is inevitably sieved
to the simple certainty
that does matter.

The Field

After Rumi: "Out beyond the ideas of wrongdoing and rightdoing there is a field."

Let's meet our selves there.

    The one who has stumbled

    and picked herself up - again.

    The one who has no fear.

Let's meet each other there.

    Leave ideas behind.

    Set wrongdoing aside.

    Even rightdoing may hush.

Let's meet in the field beyond,

our selves and each other, enlightened

by sun's rays and night's stars.

    Sit side by side.

    Feel the generous breeze.

    Touch the sweet enduring grass.

Let's thrive.

*

HANNAH MCGRAW-DZIK

Exposure

Afternoon sun-light
chooses a single leaf on a plant
just inside the door.

I see that leaf,
its veins, nourishment
throbbing through them.

One leaf on a tall plant
transparent in its exposure
like the thinnest of gossamers.

I see the leaf's veins,
my pulse throbbing in rhythm,
our rivers of life as one.

For just that instant,
the sun 's angle,
the leaf,

my awareness,
connect us together,
the one with the other.

The sun moves
the leaf turns deep green
but I have seen its veins.

I believe!

Monday Morning Matins

An open field of
cone flowers, daisies,
sway in a slight breeze,

cabbage white flies low over the grasses
monarch's wings move in and out rhythmically,
coyote scat moist underfoot.

Ant on the stem of a cattail
tiny emerald bug crosses my path,
going where, to meet whom?

Walking into wonder
sun on my face, birds chirping,

Morning prayer is done.

Uninvited Guest

In memory of my sisters, Grace, Julie, and Padraigin

Sorrow boldly knocks on my door.
Uninvited she walks in,
goes upstairs,
chooses a room in my house.

Sorrow re-arranges my furniture,
places a box of treasures
on the pine chest
lighting a candle and waits.

"How dare you invade my home."
I scream up the stairs.
"Get out-get out,
damn you, dark night of my soul."

I hear the wooden floor creak
as she rocks.
My tears come.
Sobbing, exhausted, I quiet.

When I am weak from fighting
I climb the stairs
bringing her warm soup
and a blanket.

Back downstairs
I sit at my kitchen table
quieting my heart and soul
trusting Sorrow's departure
will come.

The day arrives when
I no longer hear her rocking
I go to Sorrow's room, she is gone.

In her place, scattered about,
lay treasured memories
of a shared life with my sisters.

I bring them to my face,
smelling of them, their presence.
I rise covered with memories,

walking out of Sorrow's room.

Garden Harvest

cherry tomato round and red
just plucked from the vine
warm in my hand
into my mouth, juicy sweet
flavored with earth, rain, sun.

America's Apartheid II

Homeless

Don't you see me
I'm the one pushing the cart
Filled with your city's junk.

Homeless

Stopped at a red light
won't look at me standing with my sign,
Vet needs money, anything will help.

Homeless

I fought your wars
Lost an arm and most of my heart
Where's my thank you?

Homeless

You think my dress is pretty
Remember it's your size 13, bright yellow
I'm a size 8 and yellow is not my color.

Homeless

I'm tired, my legs are swollen
I find a place to sit and rest, I hear
move on, move on, get out of here.

Homeless

I thought our Statue of Liberty said,
"give me your tired."
Where the hell are the clean sheets and bed.
Homeless

I wait outside of restaurants
waiting for food
food that you were too full to finish.

Homeless

Along freeways, under bridges,
in an alley, my home,
all are welcome.

Bountiful

Fertile, autumn fields
produce golds of every hue
quietly waiting for the harvest.

She is pregnant, lying in a bean bag chair
her dark-haired daughters on each side.
As she reads, they listen, curled into her,
while another pulses in her rounded womb.

Soon the fields will release their bounty,
sending wealth to kitchen tables.
Through the winter the fields rest,
returning to their rich black self.

Book closed, the girls scurry to bed,
she tucks them in with a kiss.
She waits for her season of harvest,
the bounty of her pulsing womb.

Being Remembered

A rabbit died last night,
soft grayish fur, scattered
in little bundles on the driveway,

closed doors and windows saved
me from hearing Rabbit cry,
screeching as death was eating it.

Are Rabbit's children waiting at home?
Was it eagle or hawk that swept down
speeding to do what's needed to survive?

Walking back to the house, sun is rising,
mail will be delivered, phone will ring,
washing clothes, making supper,

all continues without Rabbit.
When death comes for me
swooping for my soul, ah yes,
all will continue without me.

Son at the Helm

Gossamer mist hung over the lake
as he helped me into his boat
and pushed us away from the dock.

We skimmed across the lake of glass,
to the distant shoreline
hoping for a morning catch.

Rod and reel in hand he showed me
the art of casting - letting go
reeling in, bringing home.

I received his compliments when
my lure hit just right,
"Perfect Mom, can't get any better."

Later he took us to a secluded bay
where we delighted in the
call of the loon, the soaring of an eagle.

At that moment,
he had become my teacher
as I yielded my place at the helm.

Crones of the Marsh

The aging Adirondack chair sits alone
on the edge of the brown, dried marsh.
She has lived through many seasons,
evident by ridges, splinters and holes.

She sits in her twilight,
patches of snow at her feet,
her feet blackening,
an omen of her impending death.

You and I are sisters
shaped by our own worlds.
I sit now on your generous lap,
seeing the fire of an evening sky,
hearing the crow, cawing the evening in.

I look towards my feet---
they are blackening.

*

WILL MOORE

Fire-Wrought

Words sputter forth, fiery molten metals,
Out from tiny pores through pierced cave shafts,
Melt into earth crust dirt soil stubble.
There bards dredge up poems, mold hidden
mysteries.

Angry flare-ups burn their flowing train
Pain burdens limp out beneath the red skies
Fear-struck words wield swords, sever heads, and
destroy enemies,
Cause endless vengeance to roll.

The One looks upon the reigning wars,
Stands steady, blocks the breach for all.
Cooling pardon pools the rain,
Offers poor pilgrims a holy bath

Thankful bards now offer up new poems,
Poems that cry from the naked earth,
No longer hid in molten lava fire

Spirited winds raise dust from the plains.
Silenced they settle manna across the rocks.
Hungry poets savor and chew holy bread.

Awake now fully nourished poets!
Cry out!

Passing Solitude

Solitude so dark so deep
I had taken you for mine to keep.

Solitude will have run
when this lonely age is done.

All persons will be one in one.
One magnificent communion

An eternal dance, we spin, we prance,
We twirl, we swirl, each boy and girl

Forever happy as we can be
throughout all eternity.

Solitude so dark so deep
I had taken you for mine to keep.

Wonderment

As I walk downstairs,
I tell myself: "There's something I must remember."
So, I switch the car keys to my shirt pocket.
Reaching the living room,
I begin to wander about my traces of memory,
Ones woven amidst that vast nervous jungle,
The network shock-full of intertwining vines.
I have climbed them many times before.
Most are as familiar as our front sidewalk
Still I find myself drawn to their alluring heights.
What is the hidden meaning up there?
What treasures still lie cloaked
below their leaves?
I lift and browse, flashlight in hand.
I finally descend from the meandering vine
to the kitchen.
Sensing the bulge of my keys in my shirt pocket
I have no idea what they are doing there.
I strain to recall but nothing pops up.
I only pray it was nothing crucial,
But if it was, that it would show itself again.

Carl's Wonderful Stunt

Pressed tight, Carl's flat nose smears our glass
Thick lens fills his black eyeglass frame
Dirty blonde wavy grows his hair
Safety plate window blocks Dad's blame

GI Bill glass is double-paned.
Its void silences Dad's rant out,
As the post-trauma flare of rage
Chills our hearts amid caustic shout

Seven round our dinner table
We tight-bound children fear our Dad
Meal done, Mom pops out, wipes Carl's smudge
His silly stunt smiles us kids glad

Carl's blue eyes see our pained faces.
He plays and tans in summer sun,
Comes as promise, our souls' escape,
A footpath green wood swift to run

Dinner done, Carl forges our trek
We follow to the brushy forest
Fly swiftly from our household wreck.

A Letter to the Lake

Our story took us
to the lake cabin
where the tale ends
on the beach
near the dock
Unfortunately
our grammar failed
the Ford turned into a run-on sentence
collapsed the dock
and finally came to a period
wet up to the windows
having erased the cabin cruiser
in its path
Sally and Gwen
were bracketed by parentheses in the car
as it sank deeper
Wally and Buck dove in
indented a paragraph to open the car doors
but were laden with writer's block
just then the protagonist triumphed
our hero in the Jeep
got the question mark cable in his hand
and interviewed the boys
they quickly responded
to the Ford's conundrum
The run-on was averted
as the punctuation
slow and sure
reformed the sentence
from out of the lake
Sally and Gwen wept over
the poignance of the poem

The family all critically edited one another
with parsed analytic reconstructions
Later over brats and burgers
they presented papers about the narrative
circling the beach fire
no one noticed
the closing sparks that landed
on the back of the cottage
dramatizing its wooden roof ablaze
they had all tragically fallen asleep
in their letter bags near the lake
so I doused the fire with my pen.

Howling Vortex

Great Plain walls
Wrapped in black silk
Mammals cluster in wigwams
Fires warm
Cozy cocoons dormant pupae

Winter rages
rips off shingles
trees blow down
blocked streets smashed cars

Maelstroms of wind
twist and spin
rounding the dwelling
jets roar
branches whistle
like waves crashing boulders asea
seething breathing
breath of Titans
blows across the plains

Billowing dusty clouds
of loose dirt
from farms
pelting barns and houses
burrowing into the boards
squeezing through cracks
like centipedes at night

Darkness spits out its venom
yielding never
no break
endless blackness

morning
eternities away
light unknown
past remembrance
midnite creeps in
stiffens sore

dances no more
trudges like a leaden foot
awaits a dawn
forgotten hidden
underground.

Oldness

Crackle, crunch, like old dry leaves
Stepped on, worn-out green
fibrous veins, the sole remains
of a colored life
now mostly ground-in soils.

No more does the workman ply his trade,
an artisan of finest craft.

So step down gingerly.
Walk into elder days,
where joints bend deformed
hips pop
knees grind
backs straighten slow,
and ache

Worst of all words fail
where once a rich broth
of variegated verbs
and nourishing adjectives,
now nary a simple noun
to bite.

The Children of August

The old dog, walking, pants in the heat.
In the afternoons, the locusts fly and grasshoppers
suddenly disappear.
Evenings: the crickets are chirping
in the gardens and grasses.
The robins are beginning to flock for a winter
hidden in the ravines.
The chickadees call out their cheeps to one another
as they find wavy perches on the slender weeds.
High up in the treetops the blue jays go invisible
while raucously cawing.
The crows keep appearing like miracles winging
their ways crazily across the Mississippi gorge.
Young eagles, recently cast from the nest,
fly about in circles high above the river ridge.
Vultures coast high above the river
looking for something dead.
The cormorant flies solo southbound
over the bridge.
The chipmunks scurry about holding their tails high
and dragging their cheeks full of nuts.
Squirrels, big green walnuts in their mouths,
sit on their haunches picking them apart.
Others spin acorns out of their caps
from the branches of the large white oaks.
Wild turkeys cluck in the creek bed
staying close to the fresh water.
Tree frogs sing in the forest while the night comes
on.

The cat lopes across the street
with a mouse in his mouth.
At the midnight hour the rabbits hop
into the park terrace gulley.
The children of August are very busy.
September, October, and November
stand in the wings.

*

BETTY BUCKLEY

Herding

My pen is a border collie.

The black and white dog circles left
                      and then right.
She surrounds the flock of sheep,
first moving them together
           then the same direction.
She circles back and forth
chasing the ones straying off on their own.
Slowly,
   steadily
she moves them to the same pasture.

My pen is a border collie.

My Name

What is a name,
other than how the world knows us?
Does our name shape or mold us?

My parents chose my name,
and someone else recorded it,
with a spelling I never learned.

Elizabeth is for formal documents,
Betty is for family, friends and fun.
And no using Lizzie for any reason.
           Ever.

Is it any wonder I ponder my name
or if I would have been somehow different
with a different name.

The Knitters

The women enter the room,
greet each other, choose a chair,
and pick up their knitting.

They begin with a prayer.
Share bits and pieces
of their recent days

The yarn caresses their hands as it moves
from the ball onto the needles
and into the loops of the fabric.

An observer might think the women
are only knitting shawls,
each a different color, size and shape.

But the shawls are reminders
to those who receive them
they are not alone,

Each a sign of love and support,
the women knit more than shawls.
They knit community.

The Gate

A wall divides the land.
Many stones of different sizes,
all from the same quarry,
together make the wall strong.

The wall contains a gate.
It is a deep rich brown,
with wood planed smooth.
And hinges that move quietly.

The gate watches both sides.
One, neatly trimmed green grass
the other, freshly plowed fields
waiting to be planted.

The gate encourages passage,
knowing each side is good.
The grass for rest.
The field for work.

The Cemetery

The cemetery sits on the edge of the prairie
with the Badlands in sight.
Mourners gather to say goodbye
to a mother, aunt and friend,
a farmer's wife.

There is nothing to stop the wind,
except a short shrub edging the cemetery.
Cactus burrs cling to shoes and pant legs,
giving testimony to the harshness of the land.

Grave markers tell of those
who came with high hopes and dreams,
ancestors who saw the land as good,
a place to raise crops and children.
But those hopes have blown away,
and the dreams have faded.

Even the congregation that built the cemetery is
gone, members dispersed to other churches.
The caretaker inherited the job from his father,
but has no child of his own to pass it on.

The cemetery has become a monument,
but who remains to tell its stories?

Waiting

The room is lined with chairs.
Another row divides the space.
Pale walls and random magazines;
nothing to help distract worry
concern, anxiety, the waiting.

Moved to another room,
this one smaller,
with fewer chairs,
but more waiting,

waiting for news,
for test results,
for a progress report.

Will the news allow
a return to what was,
or will it mean a move
to a new normal?

Or just more waiting.

Pay Attention

The fields were prepared for winter,
the wind changed from west to east
but experts said it was just an aberration,
and would soon return to normal.

While the snow was falling,
the easterly wind became a breeze
but experts said it was just a rarity,
and would soon return to normal.

When the snow started to melt,
the wind grew a little stronger
but experts said it was an oddity,
and would soon return to normal.

When the seeds started to sprout,
the wind grew stronger still,
but experts said it was an anomaly,
and would soon return to normal.

When the summer heat prevailed,
the wind was now a constant,
but experts said it was unprecedented,
and would soon return to normal.

After the crops where harvested,
the wind was a gusting hurricane.
The experts wondered:
When did the wind direction change?

*

HOWARD MILLER

I Write

When a tiny star grain drifts
through my open shell
and settles into the waiting nacre
like it knows what's coming,
When antagonists angrily ply my bark
      Sparking placid final amber flows,
When in an unannounced moment, joy
flies out of my mouth
      Like a bubbly faux pas,
Or equally unexpected I see death
wink across the room
      Sharing a delicious joke,
When a mirror-on-mirror wormhole
reveals suddenly,
    briefly
     the endless co-occupation of space and time,
       micro and macro worlds,
         the mindfulness of God;

I write.

Mind Voices

Why do we get so lost within ourselves?
Our eyes turned in with fear so tightly wrought;
As if within, our searching spirit delves
Solely in loss so deep it bans all thought.
We think we hear commandments from within
Which like lost spirits or wild angels sound,
Admonishing us to avoid some sin
Or other evil ends we should confound.
Why can't these voices be encouragement,
Calm whispered hints directing us through life,
Instead of a pathologic loss of sense,
Or a threshold to intense, unending strife?

With Occam's razor firmly in our fist
Why not seek truth, rather than slice our wrist?

Ages of Grace

Grace was first like a favored aunt
Who arrived unannounced,
Bustled silkily in the front hall
And then was gone
Leaving gifts and seashells in her wake
And whispers of chamomile.

Grace came again in adolescent times
When most all was indiscernible;
She slipped in with a silver click,
An impossible wink,
Showed the truth in a flash,
Then slipped out like a whisper
between belief and reality.

Now we are more frequent friends
As I embrace inevitable ends
And stay still enough to sense the thrum
Of her all but inaudible, spherical hum
In the wings of bees and birds
And the sacred sluice of words.

Cinema Verite'

Holding your hand,
I rediscover words and wordlessness in you.
Your eyes ignite my memory,
spark wild, word petals
to burst on dreaming stems.
I dance in your arms dense with tension
and fall over cliffs I'd forgotten
into swooping, giddy streams of bliss
so pleased to let go-
and dearly die in your kiss
that tomorrow doesn't care.

When the lights rise after the credits
we pull on our coats,
and edge down the sticky aisle
past the great, colorless
screen, and go
into the night,
wordless.

The Night My Mind
Was Full of You

The night my mind was full of you
would not pass quickly.
I blamed a sore neck, heat,
old favorite songs on the radio,
for my unquiet mind,
unfairly.

The years with you, digested but untasted
played out on my eyelids
as if before they could enter my dreams
I had to really live and
feel them.

Why now? Why not then?
What had we not shared?
What had you not felt?
What would I have said
if I'd been awake to you then,
Not now at 4 a.m. with you
a world and years away?

If you were here though, you'd be mad,
not at the irony of missed moments
but because I'd wakened you.

Love Aging

I want to go together ever,
over uncrossed thresholds,
to years we haven't been;
and be forever there
with you and with no other.

Our tale, tempered by years in stride,
passed worlds and sweet pastimes,
scarred though it may be by words
sometimes loosed in rage,
we are intact, on every page.

That we can weather all we are,
survive our lunacies,
horizons are passing breezes
and forever but a bar
we'll cross at leisure when it comes.

Wonderland

We are winding slowly toward the falling sun.
Though it's setting fast,
we greet each tree and bush
wind-whirled into gentle runes,
arched, storm-woven into figures
that waken in the advancing dark
shuffling roots moving among frogs and ferns
under the watery reflection
of day's end.

The granite path we know will lead
finally to a scene of soundless violence:
where bus-big blocks of granite
rest exhausted after some forgotten tumult,
content now in the pink evening,
ignoring gull hectoring
and our hushed laughter.
We sip wine and savor the last crust of sun,
murmuring disbelief about the Atlantic's brutality
that swept, unhindered by barrier islands
to fashion this headland of impossible beauty.

The Pulse, Orlando 2016

Hate is born and thrives on what is not there.

What's true is love, right before us/
Shocking beauty
dancing wild from Cadiz
haunted with cellos
harps and violas.
Its green's all around;
woods and gardens
buzzing with ruby-throats,
and bird love trilling;
flinging leaves in our path.
After each Sweet rain
clouds gild themselves.
Each day flows seamless
into a satin night
wild with moons and stars.

But we sense only our lonely angst:
others have more,
two men are kissing,
terrorists are rowing to Lesbos,
others here to replace us!

I get my gun.

Snow Tanka

Snow fell before dawn,
unmarked by mouse or bird foot
calligraphy, clear;
chiding me for my despair
at a still unwritten page.

*

SANDY NESVIG

Dilettante

Once I fancied myself a painter,
sneaking down the basement stairs
losing myself in images
stepping back to gauge my progress.
But the colors became muddy
and canvases lay unstretched.

Then there were novels,
a page or two a day,
no brushes to clean
or tubes to dry out.
But I grew tired of stealing people's lives
and unpublished manuscripts
winked knowingly of failure.

A poem is a wispy thing,
makes no demands
needs no audience
yet satisfies the desire
to let loose daily thoughts and cares
and drown the clatter
to concentrate only
on words.

The Garden

The soil is dry and cracked.
Rocks and tree roots
lie just below the surface.
Still, I plant the garden.

We will have fresh-cut flowers
in the center of the dinner table.
Once room for four,
now the two of us alone,
staring across the zinneas
and shasta daisies.

When I was younger
a garden was superfluous,
my mother's world
filled with strange names.
Hot, sweaty work and
Grime caked fingernails.

The children left,
first one and then the other,
transplanted miles away,
rooted elsewhere.

So I kneel in my garden,
Pulling weeds and propping up
the red velvet snapdragons,
snipping wilted buds, making room
for new growth.

Communion

Seven days before she died,
she baked two pies and called me
to come to dinner.

The table was set with placemats, not lace,
we drank wine and ate roast beef.
The conversation bright, memories
of countless meals salted the evening.

Somehow I knew this would be the last supper
so I stayed the night and made the calls.
The family came to say good-by
and the priest anointed her.

Her pain subdued by morphine,
she sat up, told stories, made us laugh
and promise to take care of one another
when her place at the table is empty.

His Stories

Dad used to tell stories
about having the first Model T
in his neighborhood,
his father's store,
and how he learned to sell
men's shirts and ties
when he was only thirteen.

He told us about
Prohibition, speakeasies and gangsters,
and how he found work during
The Great Depression.

Chuck and I sat at his feet
on the green footstool
and heard about
Pearl Harbor and concentration camps.
We were five and seven
and Dad knew everything.

But then we learned
that history came in books
and social studies classes.
Television gave us
pictures and *You Are There* reality.

Dad sat alone,
read *Time Magazine*
and watched Ed Sullivan.

Vigil

I have been waiting
    Staring out windows
    at winter skies, heavy grey skies
    sunless days go on and on.

I have been waiting
    Passing time in rooms,
    through hallways, tunnels, one room to the next -
    Gonda, Charlton, Jacobson and Mary Brigh.

I have been waiting
    Praying for good results
    news of negative tests
    positive procedures.

I have been waiting
    Reading newspapers in lobbies
    disheartened, angry, perplexed
    waiting for change that may not come.

I have been waiting.

Ambivalence

After Carl Sandburg and ee cummings

Spring comes
on muddy dog feet
azure days
followed by grey
skies like worn out sheets
flapping on clotheslines.

Sometimes spring brings
Hope
Renewal
Resurrection
Puddleicious memories of youth.

Othertimes
the weight of winter
hangs heavy
and spring longs for gone.
Forever.

Indian Summer

The sun rests lower in the sky.
The streets are quiet.
Sunday morning,
and leaves drift
down the sidewalks.
The air is warm,
Indian Summer
heavy with closings.

I dream of youth,
retell my father's stories,
compare myself to my mother.

This autumn is no
different than
other Octobers.
Except my house is
empty and
today I long for summers past
and dread the winter.

October 23rd

The rain soaked leaves
no longer crackle underfoot.
The elms are barren
the oak near naked.

The leaves no longer
flutter to the ground
like golden butterflies.

They drop,
heavy,
burdened with
thoughts of winter
lying ahead.

Evening Ritual

At night I pull the drape,
shut out the glow of city light,
darken the room so sleep will come.

I recite by rote childhood prayers,
repeat the litany of those
sick or saddened,
hoping the magic will heal as together
we travel the narrowing path of age.

The last name spoken,
I am at peace
able to forget that journey until
the morning sunshine
creeps in through shuttered window
and the pilgrimage continues.

*

VICTOR KLIMOSKI

Writing Poems

When poems settle down,
stake their claim on paper
or ride on a gust of breath,
they are no longer private.
They step out in public,
wear a red vest or blue top hat.
We notice them,
          walk toward them,
eager to discover what gold
they sewed in the lining of their jackets
or tucked safely in the heel of their shoes.
We listen to their stories,
the adventure they had
coming across the open plain
or through an enchanted forest.
We know all the details aren't exact:
some are for context,
          others add a splash of color.
But we lean in close,
knowing what they say
     gets better
          with each telling.

Embracing Stillness

To hear the word,
the inspired word you seek,
you must be still,
must tame the chatter
that runs like a wild child
down the corridors of your mind,
turning this way, then that,
as flashes of light catch its eye.

Stillness lies in choosing silence,
settling into its soft embrace
and, by an act of will,
finding a center point,
much as one seeks the horizon
to cross an angry sea.

When you gain equilibrium,
no longer tossed to and fro
by the turmoil of your thoughts,
you are ready to hear
what your heart wants to say,
how it tells of the wisdom
you encounter each day,
      then forget,
lost in the sound of footsteps
rushing down the hall.

The Uncluttered Mind

Before my mind is overcome
by news of the world's woe,

I want to think of water,
fresh, cold water, cascading

over shelves of jagged rock
and falling like skeins of rich silk.

As water crashes to the ground,
I want to feel its spray,

the misty baptism shriving me
of pettiness and a closed heart.

Refreshed and born again
into the heart of matter itself,

I want to embrace the world,
to let it know it is part of me

as it is part of the pooling water,
reflecting the clear blue sky.

Spring Vigil

Had we kept vigil,
we might have seen
the moment the red buds
let loose their joy,
sent out a thousand kisses,
as pursed lips,
opened slowly
to reveal pink little tongues
ready to sing the Sun awake.

Awakening

When a day opens
as perfect as this one
like a wild blue iris
with petals of silk
and an elegant neck
wrapped in drops of dew;
or as perfect as this trail,
winding through the woods,
its very emptiness
tracing a graceful line;
or as perfect as the fist of wrens
moving from place to place
across the frosted lawn
in bursts of energy
we long to harness.

On as perfect a day as this,
let anxiety seep into the ground
and all fear stay outside the door,
like boots we'd leave
after crossing a muddy field.

Speaking Marriage

Marriage is a language with its own grammar,
complicated as Gaelic, with a vocabulary
as layered in meaning as Cantonese.
Fluency takes diligence, but we settle for dialect
picked up on the streets, content it's enough
even when it sounds like the broken English
my foreign grandmother spoke.

We stitch together phrases, thinking our point made
when what we actually said lacks a proper predicate
and uses the pluperfect when present tense is best.
Or we say "whatever" intending neutrality
while the other hears indifference.

A basic literacy test before we're licensed to wed,
or a phrase book kept in a breast pocket,
might spare us tripping over our twisted tongues.
Even better would be a Google app
able to conform a response to it truest meaning
before it leaves our mouths.

Sorrow's Journey

Sorrow pulls up its heavy woolen cowl,
folds its hands into draped sleeves,
and walks, head down, step by step,
the long, cold corridor of grief.

Sorrow stops from time to time,
as though marking Stations of the Cross.
At each stop Sorrow sings its lament,
its voice rending the heart's silence.

Sorrow paces up and down, all day long,
the echo of its footsteps a painful cadence
interrupting the fragile attempt to sleep
and escape from the haunt of memory.

At a time unnamed and undated,
Sorrow slips out unnoticed.
What lingers is the sound of its pacing
and the fading strains of its lament.

The Tainted Origin of Vocation

At thirteen I had a vision,
well, if not a vision, a notion,
if not a notion, a sudden whim
I would become a priest.
My mother thought it odd
for one whose moods
could curdle milk,
but believing in miracles
(and having a priest of her own),
she began sewing my name
on new underwear from Penney's.

My father thought the idea obscene,
a child living away from home,
growing up among strangers.
But then we argued over chores
for the hundredth time in a week,
and he decided who was he
to question the will of God.

Love Ye Therefore the Stranger
(Deuteronomy 10:19)

When we look at them,
faces formed like our own,
the notion of difference shifts.
Recognizing ourselves in them
      and them in us,
changes the story we tell,
for we hold parts in common
though told from different angles
of birth, origins, and language.

We follow different stars,
face different crossroads,
suffer different perils.
What from afar seems so alien,
close up refines our sight
and compels us to draw near,
for their lives are not incidental,
and so differently composed,
we've nothing to learn
      or love.

Seeing God

No one has seen God
except the blue heron
standing in silent awe
at the edge of the lake.
The heron never blinks
or turns its head
to see what else is near.
Once you've seen God,
you never wonder
where to look next.

LINDA THAIN

What Poems Can Accomplish

I.
I excavate.
Dust off.
Scrub.
Examine.
Patch.
Enliven.
Burnish.

In order to
Define.
Refine.
Honor.

Clothe rather than accessorize.
Enjoy rearranging to reveal what belongs.

II.
I Illuminate.
Clarify.
Elucidate.
Reflect.
Lighten.
Brighten.
Finally, lacquer.

Revise.
Renew.
Re-learn.
Repair.
Re-imagine.

Cast glitter, not shadows.

Curate the light.
Tell my own story.

III.
This morning
Bare branches
Frame our piece of the sky.
I resent the Spring leaves
that will obscure that view.

Winter has suited me well this year.

This evening
A Spring poem
Starts to bloom.

The beginning of my reconciliation with change.

IV.
It is enough to see.
It is possible to note
Every detail.
To illustrate the importance
Of praising what is there
Without trying to figure it out.

V.
Letting go.
Splintered, dissolved, diffused.
Is all the light lost
Or is it merely repurposed?

The Kaleidoscope turns
For another brief view.

Be prepared to turn it again.
Soon.

Illuminating, coloring, reflecting.
Recharging while
Holding on to the source.

Why the Track
and Not the River Path?

I follow the rabbit onto
The black bitumen 6-lane oval.
Can he explain the arcane green rectangles
and red arrows?
Or what the red circles in lane 5 designate?

Butterfly.
Halloween black and orange.
Sunshine yellow.

Bird.
Red belly.
Madonna blue body and wings.

Feather.
Striped.
A marker from an eagle?
A turkey?

Dried grasses available for nests.
Two green shoots
Escape through the seemingly solid surface.

Seeds of poems push up
From the monotony underfoot
To the unobstructed sky.

Retired Teacher

For many years in my classroom
The first student assignment.
An essay on your favorite season.

My exemplar.
"My favorite season is fall because…"

In five paragraphs I praised
Crisp blue skies,
Long walks,
Changing leaves.

Today I walk.
A couple unload three pumpkins
Under calling geese framed by a perfect sky.
Yellow leaves camouflage
Streets, sidewalks, and cars.
A classic red brick school waits.
Its doors locked.

At the halfway mark
A cream scone and coffee.

Tomorrow.
No door to unlock
On a carefully curated classroom.

Is Fall still my favorite?

Meditations:
Minneapolis Institute of Art

1. *9 x 9 x 9 - Mona Khartoum*
*Youth Book Tour - 2015 - <u>The One and Only Ivan</u> - Katherine
Applegate*

In the gallery the children and I confront
The barbed wire
ten foot cube.

I find the page.

Ivan, a silverback gorilla.
Finally freed from 23 years
In a glass and metal cage.
12 X 12 X 12.

I read out loud.

Sky.
Grass.
Tree.
Ant.
Stick.
Bird.
Dirt.
Cloud.
Wind.
Flower.
Rock.
Rain.
Mine.
Mine.

Mine.

When the cage door opens
What do the artist,
The author,
The readers
Hope for?

2. ***The Bwa Mask - Artist Unknown***

The African Plank Mask.
12 feet of black, red, and white painted wood.

After years of study,
Wisdom is passed from elders to youth.

I explain to the children that the wearer
Completely encases his body in a raffia suit.

A little boy stands
Letting go of his father's hand
For the first time on the tour,
"That's because the spirits are so powerful."

The spirits find a perch
In masks, statues, paintings, words.

We find protection.

3. *Night Sky #6* - Via Clemens

Via Clemens spent years
Painting layers, sanding them down, repainting.
Not tedious - a chance to be part of the Night Sky.

She made millions of decisions.
It takes the viewer just seconds to accept the
invitation.

We might think removing a mistake
Gives us a chance to start over.
Try burnishing it.

4. *Blessing of the Tuna Fleet* - Paul Signac

A safe journey.
A bountiful harvest.
A welcoming port.
The scene illuminated.

Step back.

Permission to adventure.
Guidance for success.
An open invitation to return.
The blessing elucidated.

Concert in St. Mary's Chapel

Saint Paul Seminary, University of St. Thomas

I try to notice details.

The Stations proclaim a story.
The floor hushes footsteps.
The ceiling draws the eye upward.
The oversize fount urges blessings.
Heavy wooden doors protect the precious colored light.

I coolly observe.

Until the sopranos hit the note
Which secures the scene
In my heart.

A Year of Heavy Lifting

I lead museum tours with a photographer.
I guide the aspiring teens as they respond
To photos documenting struggles for human rights.
My colleague teaches techniques which will allow
Them to observe through the lens of a camera.

He describes himself as Intersectional.

He is black, adopted by white parents.
He is GLBTQ.
He fits nowhere.
Or is it everywhere?

50 years older, I see myself in his description.

I am WWF (Widowed White Female).
Finding ways to strengthen myself
For the daily wrestling match
To move my heavy heart
Through the intersection between grief
And appreciation for blessings.

Grief at the Loss of My Husband

Pictures on the bookcase.
I know what's behind each smile.
I now work to reinvent mine.

Your sister's ringtone.
It's for you.
I have to answer.

I step on the bathmat
Without drying my feet.
No need to keep it dry.

White tulips in February.
In my newly purchased vase.
They wilt.

A hundred cards, emails, assurances.
"You're doing all the right things."
It helps a little.

A friend had to go to the dermatologist
After her husband died.
I check each morning for tear tracks.

Unexplored territory.
A church discussion group.
I see myself in a parable.

Enjoying new experiences.
Talking to new people.
I need to practice going to the grocery store.

I scrub the pots.
Aspiring to your standard of cleanliness.
Honor in a can of Bar Keepers Friend.

Four years ago treasures were downsized.
With no place to hang memories
Can they survive?

Betrayed by frozen blueberries.
Will your leftover bag bring me a longer life?
It's worth a try.

A postponed call to VISA.
A cancelled credit card
Is so final.

Waiting with a friend at her doctor.
They call, "Richard."
You aren't there.

I used to go out without
A tissue tucked in
Every pocket.

Each time I left home you said
"Have fun. Take care."
I say it now for both of us.

Your choice made to stop oxygen.
You say, "Do you think it will be fun?
Take care.

*

CONTRIBUTOR NOTES

BETTY BUCKLEY (b. 1955, St. Paul MN) is a retired Civil Engineer who worked for the Minnesota Department of Transportation for 33 years. She started to develop her creative side by knitting for herself and for charity. She took a basket making class on a whim, enjoyed it and now travels throughout the Midwest to take classes. Her family is the beneficiary of her baskets. A couple of years into retirement, she decided to try the workshop on writing at the Selim Center of the University of St. Thomas. In poetry she has found a new creative way to capture her thoughts. This is her first published set of poems.

VICTOR KLIMOSKI (b. 1945, Langlade WI), an educator by professional training, is a writer by aspiration. Over the past thirty years he has been composing a daily poem or, as often is the case, assembling words in hope of shaping an idea he encountered on his morning walk, in his reading, and in conversations that trigger the glimmer of an image. Workshop opportunities over the years with master writers have been developed both his creative and critical skills. Several years ago, he discovered that assembling collections of poems honed his skills for revision, sharpening his ear for what he was really trying to say. He convenes workshops and retreats to support, encourage, and, where he can, guide other writers. His most recent collection is *Margin Notes* (Amazon, 2017) and a major revision and editing of his first collection, *A Month In Kilcar*, will be released in January 2018.

HANNAH MCGRAW-DZIK E.B.N. (b. 1941, Stewart MN) grew up on a farm and close to nature from birth. So close so, she claims the title of "education by nature" when she writes poetry. Married, mother, grandmother, great-grandmother, and lover of life. She was a gatherer of eggs, setter of bowling pins, X-ray technician, waitress, book seller, and the last 40 years a storyteller known as the Shoeless Storyteller. "I write poetry to be delighted and to discover. I search for my truth, who was I created to be, what legacy will I leave for those that I love so deeply. Those answers are sometimes found in a simple poem about a dead rabbit or a homeless person."

SHEILA MARTIN (b. 1956, Grand Rapids MN) has been writing down poems since 2005, after three heart attacks, when the right side of her brain was suddenly released from captivity. Since then, her lens on life has improved tremendously, and her life-long love of words has found creative expression in many forms. Sheila's poems emerge out of reverence for the natural world, life discoveries and predicaments, and her increasingly personal spiritual meanderings. Ms. Martin is grateful for the midwifery of the Writers Consortium, for helping her release some poems from their frayed folders. In New Brighton Minnesota, where she lives with her immensely patient life partner, Chris, she is working on more poems to share.

HOWARD MILLER (b. 1948, Piqua OH), until becoming a member of this consortium, wrote poems only erratically. Typically writing in moments of despair or joy, poems were therapeutic or a means to other ends. Involvement in this consortium provided discipline while adding new vistas of what a muse could be. Experiences from a life in service to people with disabilities, especially those with mental illness, provide a didactic tone to several of his poems in this collection. A lifelong love of the arts, especially works from the Romantic period, lends some works a colorful, even melodramatic tone fitted into traditional poetic forms. Wife Kate, life and travel companion, is omnipresent in his work.

WILL MOORE (b. 1951, St. Paul MN). Of old I kept journals to lend solidity to the storms within my mind and heart. Most entries divulged my character flaws with repeated resolutions to amend. Occasionally I'd write letters to people I hated or who'd wounded me. I'd never send them. I wrote to vent like punching the bag. Being a registered nurse, I approach matters scientifically: observe, assess, plan, act, evaluate and reassess day after watchful day. I've switched now to the humanities and theology to create and write about who I am, who God is, and what's our relationship? Over the years as a learner in a variety of settings, I developed shorthand to help find the gist of the complex. Now my poems tend to be on the terse side. They express only the central seed shown in the heart of earth language that needs adornment.

SANDY NESVIG (b. 1947, Fargo ND) didn't do much creative writing (except for a few poems expressing deep adolescent angst!) until leading a writers workshop for seventh and eighth graders. Her participation in the Minnesota Writing Project led her to believe it was not reasonable to expect students to write forty minutes each day and not do so herself. She also joined a writers' group that sprang from the Writing Project. Needing to share once a month is a great motivator. However, the group disbanded, and she left the classroom for administration, and poetry was on hiatus. After retirement she was delighted when the Selim Center at the University of St. Thomas offered a summer session on memoir and poetry. It was even better when the group continued to meet. Some of the poems here are a result of assignments for the group and some come from the years of teaching.

LINDA THAIN (b. 1947, Chicago IL) taught Middle School in the Saint Paul Public Schools for 35 years. She often was pleased with the pieces she wrote to serve as examples for her students. Encouraged by these efforts, she occasionally took writing classes and enjoyed the bursts of energy with which she completed assignments. Until participating in this year-long workshop, she never had the discipline to establish a regular writing practice. After a year in which her life required major revision she's relished the chance to move from teacher to student. She's discovered the satisfaction of uncovering unknown layers of feeling as, with the help of the group, she burnished her poems.